Charlotte Mia Legnano

ACTIVITY BOOK *for* BETRAYED WOMEN

REBUILD YOUR SELF-ESTEEM AFTER BEING CHEATED ON

Hello,
wonderful being !

I know perfectly well what is going on in your life right now.

You've entered the **"shock-gap"**. The discovery of your beloved's selfishness is such an unexpected twist that it's blown a hole in your sense of certainty and left a huge gap between your expectations and reality.

Your normal is out of control. This type of thing is so painful, it radically upsets the balance of things and leaves you living with a new out of control normal.

You've lost your confidence. You no longer feel certain of the things you used to be certain about, and since you no longer control what normal feels like, your self-confidence, your sense of security, and your self-esteem take a beating.

This book is for you...

If you've recently had your heartbroken, your trust violated, your dreams disappointed, but you refuse to let the hurt drag you down any longer.

This book is for everyone...

Who's ever experienced the pain of being betrayed, lied to, or played falsely by someone they trusted, and yet they reject the idea of growing old bitter and chained to fear, doubt and mistrust.

My hope is to turn these written words into an escalator back to peace for anyone who's been through hell but refused to take permanent residence there. If this sounds like something you want, then let's get to it.

Here's my promise to you:
I promise that when you finish this book you'll look in the mirror and smile at the amazing person who overcame that painful bump in the road like a champion. Betrayal is such a hard experience that it requires overwork. With this book:

You will overcome the trauma of betrayal and regain self-confidence. You will rebuild self-esteem and spend valuable time alone with yourself. You will find inspiration and hidden messages here. You will do tasks that free your creativity and rebuild your imagination. You will find space in this book to create a new vision of the future. You will find solace and peace to go deeper into yourself.

You will mentally prepare yourself to open up to a new love. You will solve logic tasks that will awaken your troubled mind. You will redefine love and rebuild yourself. You will begin to affirm. You will awaken the artist in you. You will do the work on yourself that will allow you to close a painful chapter. You will redirect attention to yourself.

As you read along, allow yourself to consider all strategies and suggestions in this book with an open mind. Remember, consideration isn't the same as acceptance. You can consider some things and discard them, and you can consider other things and accept them. The key is to accept only those things you believe can move you closer to your goals. Can you do that? (I know you can).

Great, then let's begin!

I'll keep my fingers crossed for you!

Charlotte Mia Legnano

And remember... true love always wins! If it doesn't, know that it wasn't real.

Betrayal
is a little **death.**

You're feeling betrayed.

It hurts.
It is devastating.

Somewhere in the recent past, you made the unpleasant discovery of your partner's infidelity and in the blink of an eye everything changed.

It's almost as if you tumbled down a rabbit hole. But rather than ending up in Wonderland, you seem to have ended up in "Horror Land," where everything is the exact opposite of the way it was before.

You never thought it would happen to you, but it has. Your partner, possibly even the love of your life, cheated on you. Someone you love has broken the bonds of trust and done something that cuts deep at your heart.

You might be numb. You might be so angry you can't even see straight. However you might be feeling, regardless of how long it has been since you found out your partner was unfaithful to you, let yourself feel it. Do not push it away or ignore it. The best thing you can do is let those feelings in.

Being cheated on is an awful experience, and it would be wrong to allow yourself to believe feeling sad or angry or hurt is not allowed. Someone you loved betrayed you. You are going to feel a lot of things you do not want to feel, but that is normal. That is acceptable. You need to process those feelings in order to heal and come back to yourself again.

When you feel betrayed, it's not something that can be dealt with too quickly. You need time to process everything that has happened and this will vary depending on the specific events.

At first, you just have to do your best to cope with the storm of emotions inside while maintaining some semblance of a normal life. After all, you still have responsibilities to take care of.

In time, you'll find you overcome the initial shock and start to heal your emotional wounds.

After experiencing trauma, coming back to confidence and peacefulness can feel overwhelming. Trauma can often separate us from feeling good in our bodies and minds, but there are ways to counter those feelings.

Give yourself
time to heal.

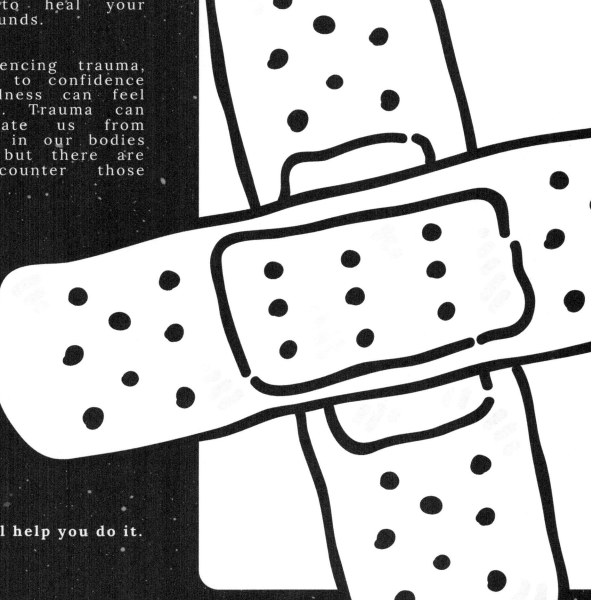

This book will help you do it.

Comforting **stats.**

Finding out that your partner cheated can make you feel rejected and isolated, but you're definitely not, and the statistics show that you'd be hard-pressed to find anyone who hasn't been cheated on.

Just knowing this may give you some type of comfort because you're one in millions of people across the world who are dealing with **this situation everyday.**

Betrayal and fraud are a real scourge of modern times. Surprisingly, the numbers also show that both men and women run neck in neck with regards to infidelity:

- Men and women both play the cheating game, with 57% of men admitting to infidelity and 54% of women admitting to the same.

- 74% of men and 68% if women say yes, they would have an affair if they knew they'd never get caught.

- Amazingly, 56% of men and 34% of women say they'd cheat even thought they're happy in their current relationships.

- There's no direct link between being unhappy in a marriage and cheating.

- The tendency to cheat may be genetic, and is linked to alcoholism, and gambling.

- 41% of marriages have either partner admitting they cheated emotionally or physically.

- 30% to 60% of married individual admitted to cheating, but that number may be low considering the fact that the very nature of infidelity is to be dishonest, and some people will be deceitful in studies conducted about being deceitful.

The tendency to ask yourself 'Why?' and desperately look to yourself for the answers is common among women who've been cheated on. Many times, the injured women will reason that it's somehow their fault; "If only I were prettier"; "If only I had a better figure"; "If only I were smarter".

Being vulnerable and picking yourself apart to find answers will damage your self-esteem even more, when the truth is, there's no rhyme or reason for infidelity. Beautiful, successful people like Jennifer Aniston, Halle Berry, and supermodel Christie Brinkley have all reportedly been cheated on. And people that you come in contact with every day; the young cashier at the store, your confident boss, the friend you go out for coffee with could be going through relationship infidelity too.

When you stand back and look at the commonality of cheating in relationships, you'll see that cheaters will cheat; they'll cheat on anyone, no matter what their significant other looks like, what their employment status is or what they did or didn't do in the relationship. You're okay the way you are, and the chance that the cheating didn't have anything to do with you is extremely high.

It's Statistically True.

Most cases of cheating are just simple, bad choices that a partner has made because the time was right, and the opportunity was there.

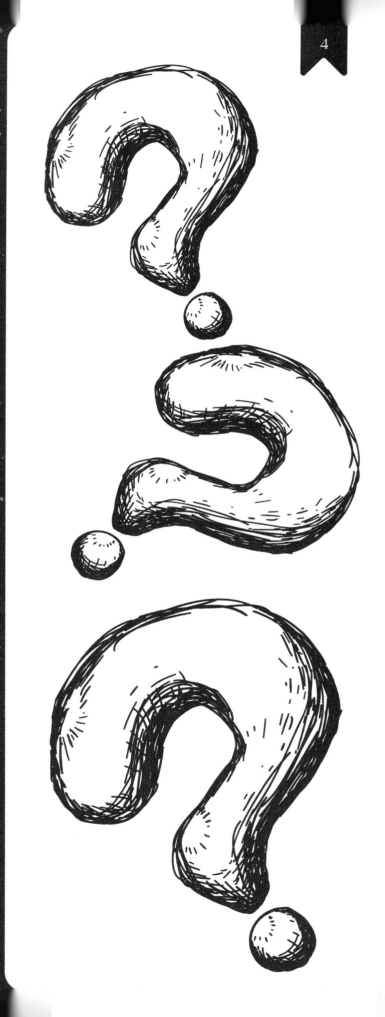

The Killer *of* **self-** esteem.

Betrayal is a direct blow to self-esteem. After the initial shock has passed, one of the most painful side effects will be the feeling that you are not attractive, intelligent or interesting.

Your self-confidence (which was in good shape the day before you discovered the betrayal) is now shattered.

There's nothing like betrayal to throw your self-esteem for a loop. When your partner betrays you, you are devastated. But, your devastation might pale in comparison to the hit that your self-esteem takes when this happens.

Infidelity is the worst of the worst when it comes to damaging your self-esteem.

However, I'm here to tell you that you can—and will —feel whole again. Remember that you're the same amazing person now that you were before the discovery of the affair.

And, with **extra self-care**, you'll be back in good shape again.

There's nothing like **betrayal** to throw your **self-esteem** for a loop.

What *is* self-esteem?

Here's a definition I like: Self-esteem is the emotional energy generated from the way you feel about yourself.

It's the fuel that powers your motivation, risk tolerance, confidence, and ability to cope with uncertainty.

I'm describing self-esteem as both "energy" and "feeling". This is because self-esteem is generated from your feelings about yourself. Think of self-esteem like the gas tank in your car.

If your overall feelings about yourself are positive, then you are full of self-esteem. If the overall feelings are negative, then your self-esteem is low. Your self-esteem energy is generated by your expectations.

Where does Self-Esteem **Energy** come from?

Positive emotions are created by positive expectations that generate healthy (or high) self-esteem. Negative emotions, created by negative expectations, drain or lower one's self-esteem.

So, where do our expectations originate? **They mostly come from our self-image.**

Betrayal tends to
negatively impact **Self-esteem**.

When something as painful as betrayal rocks your world, it generally does two things:

- It unleashes a tremendous amount of negative stress into your life.
- It triggers the fear of future pain.

And it's this fear of future pain that robs you of self-esteem energy. Why? Because as I already pointed out, self-esteem energy is generated from positive expectations.
And what happens when you're afraid of future pain?

That's right! That generates negative expectations, which in turn lowers your self-esteem. Remember, I told you that expectations (negative or positive) are largely created by our self-image? Now it's time to talk about how important a role your self-image plays.

Self-image is the Key to Self-esteem.

What is self-image?

Self-image is the foundation upon which you build your entire personality, behaviors and expectations.

And here's how Dr. Maltz described self-image in his groundbreaking book "Psycho-Cybernetics":

"Whether we realize it or not each of us carries about with us a mental blueprint or picture of ourselves (our self-image).

It is built up by our beliefs about ourselves, and it is 100% complete, right down to the last detail that tells us 'this is the sort of person I am.' We do not question its validity but proceed to act upon it just as if it were true."

Bottom line?

A person's self-image is a composition of all the opinions, beliefs, superstitions and approximations they've adopted about themselves. This tells us that self-image is a story you've created about who you are, what's possible and what's not possible for you, what you can and can't do, and what's acceptable and unacceptable to you.

Beauty *and* ugliness.

We must do a great deal of re-framing. First of all, there is the old adage that beauty is as beauty does. You were the one who remained loyal to your marriage, held up the family in times of crises, lived your life as an honorable woman, and remained a good wife or partner. That is beautiful!

The truth is that age and experience define all that is beautiful. How we live our lives well defines beauty. Kindness to others defines beauty.

In it's pure essence, beauty is internal and it can be seen in the soul, which shines through your eyes. Beauty is something that you do on a daily basis and beauty is shown through your actions.

In fact, your partner's betrayal should stand in stark contrast to all that you are and all that you stand for. You were the one who kept constant integrity. That's beautiful. You were the one who took the high road and chose to be a good wife or girlfriend. That's beautiful. You live a life where you do not hurt others. That's beautiful.

Contrast that to the person who betrayed you. It doesn't matter what his exterior might look like, I can guarantee that , he is an ugly human being. he is a wretched creature who chose to disrupt the beauty of the family and the sanctity of marriage or partnership. That's ugly. He chose to lie, to be selfish, to pursue something that went about shattering lives in secret. That's pure ugliness.

Beauty is as **beauty** does.

5 Tips *for*
Dismantling
Self-Doubt
&
Increasing
Self-Confidence
after cheated on.

#1
Don't Believe Everything
You Think.

Just because a thought, idea, or belief is in your mind, it doesn't mean it's true. Be willing to look at all thoughts... question every premise... and discard all the shabby ones.

From today forward, give yourself permission to rethink any negative expectations... any belief that suggests any lack or limitation... and any idea that tries and undermines your faith in the future.

#2
Opinions Should Never Be
Treated as Facts.

It would give me great joy for you to recognize that opinions (even your own) are not facts.

It's important to understand that a fact is immutable, while an opinion is not. Therefore, all opinions (including your own) should never be given too much of a superior position in your mind. In other words, it's OK to doubt your own self-doubts.

They are just opinions.

#3
Unpleasant Memories Need
Never Be Relived.

The best thing about the past is that it's over. It's gone. This is a fact, not an opinion. The only way the past comes back is if you relive it in your mind. Why do so many of us relive the past over and over again? People believe that by reliving a past unpleasantness, they will gain the power to prevent it from happening again. But when you look at this belief rationally, you'll find it doesn't make much sense. It would be like sticking your hand in an electric socket over and over again to remind yourself not to stick your hand in an electric socket!
Forget about that.

The past is over. There's no need to relive it. (Because the deeper lessons aren't learned from pain but from insight.)

#4
Changing Your Mind Is Your
Privilege as An Adult.

This is my favorite part of being an adult: No one tells you who you are. (You're the one telling yourself who you are.) And the best part of being an adult is the freedom to change your mind about who you are and what's possible for you. If you find you're lacking faith in yourself, then it's your privilege to change your mind about yourself and about what you're capable of.

Keep in mind, the stories you tell yourself about yourself are the wood for the fire of self-doubt or the fire of self-confidence. So, make sure you only add fuel to the one you want to grow.

#5
Shift Your Focus from Loss to Learning.

I believe there's always a way to turn any adversity into an advantage. Every single negative can lead to a positive. And one way to jump-start this process is to shift your focus from what you've lost to what you've learned.

Here's what this means:

Rather than looking, focusing or obsessing on the things you lose in any situation, adversity or crisis... I want you to shift your attention to the lessons you've learned.

Now, the experience becomes a teaching device, not a torture device. And at that moment, you awaken a power within yourself that transforms that which was sent to curse you into that which has come to bless you.

Once you've experienced this power for yourself, a new level of confidence is awakened... as you realize that you now have the capacity to handle whatever curveballs life throws at you. This power is called resiliency, and it's an antidote to self-doubt and the precondition to self-confidence. So, go ahead and shift your focus from loss to learning and awaken that power now.

Your self-esteem and self-confidence are gifts given from you to you, and they're gift wrapped in the stories and images you believe about yourself.

Two things to keep in mind about your gift:

Nothing outside of you increase or decrease your value.

There's no limit on how much you can increase in value.

Things You Need To Know About **Repairing Self-Confidence** After Betrayal

What is self-confidence?

Self-confidence is the belief that you can and will get your needs met.

When you have self-confidence, it's because you believe that you have the necessary resources to handle whatever emerges.
Self-confidence is what gives us the faith that we can solve problems, tolerate risks, bounce back from adversity, recover from loss, and surrender to change.

How does self-confidence look like?

It shows up in your life as faith in yourself, self-assurance, self-reliance, personal power, fearlessness, resiliency, and (believe it or not) confidence in your own ability to learn.

What is the opposite of self-confidence?

Self-doubt, which is a lack of faith in yourself and your ability to get your needs met.

How does infidelity affect self-confidence?

Although many things can trigger self-doubt, the discovery of betrayal (or feeling played for a fool) has got to be at the top of the list. So, how does self-doubt after betrayal manifest itself?

Self-doubt after betrayal shows up in two key ways:

Lack of faith in your ability to prevent a future betrayal

Lack of faith in your own ability to handle possible future pain
The Worst Part? Your self-doubts can be crueler than the worst of their lies.

So, how do you rebuild self-confidence after you've been cheated on?

Here's the secret: You don't focus on rebuilding confidence... you focus on removing doubt. That's right. Rebuilding confidence is actually a process of undoing, more than it is a process of doing. Unfortunately, many people miss this key point because if you were to try and rebuild your confidence without first dismantling self-doubt, it would be like rebuilding a house using just straw. All it would take is for one Big Bad Wolf to huff and puff and blow all your self-confidence to smithereens.

So, let's take the bull by the horns and learn how to pull out those weeds of self-doubt so that confidence grows back naturally. Because in the end, the only security is the courage to trust yourself.

Are you ready to **rebuild your self-esteem** after being betrayed?

yes   no

Are you ready to work **through trauma?**

yes   no

Are you ready to start the **greatest new chapter** in your life?

yes   no

If you answered **YES** three times then we can get started!

Choose intuitively the task you will perform today.
Choose one of the symbols you like and then go to the designated page.

14

WHEEL OF LIFE

The wheel of life is a great tool that helps you better understand what you can do to make your life more balanced. Think about the 8 life categories below, and rate them from 1 - 10.

PERSONAL GROWTH

HEALTH

FINANCE

FRIENDS

CAREER

RELATIONSHIPS

SPIRITUALITY

RECREATION

1 2 3 4 5 6 7 8 9 10

COLORING THERAPY

1 / 15

Mental stress is detrimental for your health, and it can lead to physical problems. If you have constant stress, then you can develop high blood pressure or digestive issues. Reduce stress by using coloring for stress relief. Rather than using food or alcohol to relieve your stress after hard times, keep an **assortment of coloring pages and beautiful crayons ready at home.**

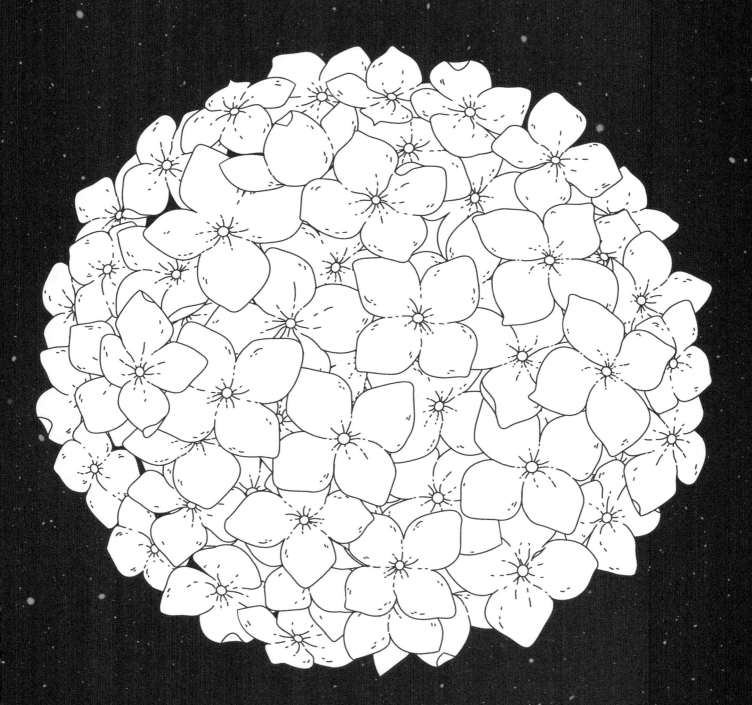

DEFINE LOVE

You likely hear references to love every day, but defining what it means can be difficult. Love means different things to different people, and you can experience different types of love depending on the situation. Decide what love means you to you. Once you understand love, you'll be able to tell when you're in love with someone.

Define love - when you define exactly what love is to you, you will be able to tell when you are truly in love with someone.

20

My definition of love and partnership

EVERY BROKEN HEART CAN BE MENDED

Every broken heart can be mended.
Find a way to fix yours.

ONLY YOU CAN DO IT

You can use a special band-aid to mend a broken heart.

YOU WILL FIND THEM IN THE LAST PAGES OF THE BOOK

EVERY FEMALE BODY IS A WORK OF ART

DIVERSITY IS BEAUTY

It's easy to lose your self-esteem when you discover betrayal. It's time to remind you how much beauty is in you.

MARK AND DESCRIBE WHAT YOU LOVE ABOUT YOURSELF
FOCUS ON PHYSICAL CHARACTERISTICS

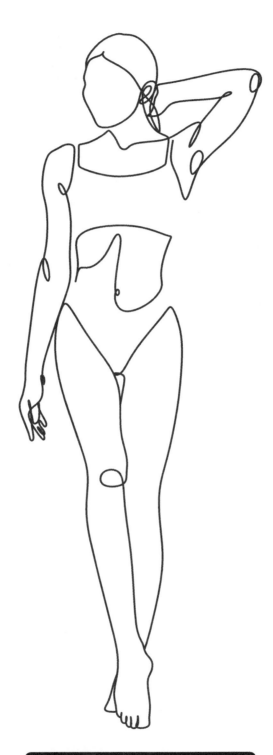

Every female body is **a work of art**.
Regardless of the current **canons of beauty**.
Be proud of **your body**.
It is perfect in **every way**.
Diversity is **beauty**.

THE
GRATITUDE
JAR

The gratitude jar is a stunningly simple exercise that can have profound effects on your wellbeing and outlook. It only requires a few ingredients: a jar (a box can also work); a ribbon, stickers, glitter, or whatever else you like to decorate the jar; paper and a pen or pencil for writing your gratitude notes; and gratitude!

Step 1: Find a jar or box

Step 2: Decorate the jar however you wish.

You can tie a ribbon around the jar's neck, put stickers on the sides, use clear glue and glitter to make it sparkle, paint it, keep it simple, or do whatever else you can think of to make it a pleasing sight.

Step 3:

This is the most important step, which will be repeated every day.

Think of at least three things throughout your day that you are grateful for. It can be something as benign as a coffee at your favorite place, or as grand as the love of your significant other or dear friend. Do this every day, write down what you are grateful for on little slips of paper and fill the jar.

Step 4: Gratitude!

DECODED
MESSAGE
GOLDEN THOUGHTS

★ ★ ★ ★ ★

" |_|_| |_|_|_|'|_|_| |_|_|_|_|_|
_	_	_	_	_	_		_	_		_	_	_
_	_	_	_	_	_	_	,	_	_	_
_	_	_	_		_	_	_	_	_	_	_		_	_	_
_	_	_	_		_		_	_	_
_	_	_	_	_	_	. "

here enter the deciphered message for you

Solve the maze and you will decode the message.

YOUR
DECALOGUE
OF LOVE

THINK ABOUT WHAT IS MOST IMPORTANT TO YOU IN A
SUCCESSFUL RELATIONSHIP

I

II

III

IV

V

VI

VII

VIII

IX

X

DECALOGUE of LOVE

DRAWING THERAPY

DRAWING CAN BE AN ACT OF SELF-CARE — RELEASING STRESS,
BOOSTING CREATIVITY, AND PROMOTING MINDFULNESS.

BOUND-
ARIES IN A
RELATION-
SHIP

Women often forgive what should not be forgiven. It's time to put boundaries. Write on the wall everything that you do not accept in a relationship. **Remember your boundaries and don't let anyone cross them.**

34

THE POSITIVE OF PAINFUL EXPERIENCES

There are tiny lessons in each experience, even if you don't realize it. Even if you think the process is not happening, not for you at least. But it is happening. It is certain. Each and every of the painful experiences has a meaning in the end.

The meaning is to show us something we must learn so we can continue down our path with a lighter burden on our back and our limits clear. When the limits of our path are not defined, we run into walls and stumble from one place to the next. On the other hand, when we build our identity and seek out what makes us fulfilled, our minds become more lucid and our roads more fertile.

Therefore, painful experiences are intimately linked with chances to learn something in life. Behind every bad experience there is a potential lesson we shouldn't overlook. Because there are situations in life that we repeat over and over again until we learn from them.

Learn from painful experience.

What can I do to prevent this from happening again?

Why am I suffering?

COLOR OF HAPPINESS

Color the picture with the colors
that you associate with happiness.

38

PRACTICE SELF-LOVE

SOLO DATE

We are afraid to be alone because we don't want to be alone with our thoughts. We need our friends, families, and significant others to save us from our own enemy — **our mind.**

It's important to strike a balance between spending the time with yourself, taking it slow, or in other words, dating yourself is just as important as it is to spend time with others in a social setting, and here is why — the more you go on dates with yourself the more you get to know yourself better and the more you start knowing yourself better the more **you love yourself.**

Start Dating Yourself & Your Whole Life Will Change.
Go on 3 dates with yourself in the next 30 days

What does it mean to date yourself?

What does it look like to start dating another person? You probably compliment them a lot, spend quality time with them, try new things with them, buy them nice things, and really get to know them. Basically, dating yourself is the same! It means devoting time and energy to nurturing your relationship with your inner self.

It doesn't matter so much what kind of solo date you take yourself on. What matters is that you spend that time in intentional solitude and start to get comfortable with yourself.

First Date With Yourself: *date: __/__/____*
A first date with yourself must be special. Make yourself divine. Put on your best clothes. Feel your femininity, dance for yourself in front of the mirror. Take some sexy selfies. Feel into yourself. Drink a glass of proseco with yourself and toast yourself.

Second Date With Yourself: *date: __/__/____*
Cook a fancy meal for yourself. Light some candles, put on some music, and tap into your inner Gordon Ramsey.

Third Date With Yourself: *date: __/__/____*
(plan your 3rd date)

....
....
....
....
....
....
....
....

NAME YOUR FEELINGS

Name your feelings.

Betrayal is an act. The emotions that result from it are what we mean when we say we're "feeling betrayed."
In order to start recovering from the act, you must be more specific about the feelings it has given rise to.

COLOR OF LOVE

**Color the picture with the colors
that you associate with love.**

LINE OF

BIRTH
0 YEARS OLD

YOUR LIFE

Below you see the lines of your life.
This line represents your entire life
from birth to death,
assuming you live to be 80 years old.

MARK THE POINT WHERE YOU ARE NOW
& PLAN THE REMAINING TIME YOU HAVE LEFT

DEAD
80 YEARS OLD

COLORING THERAPY

2 / 15

Mental stress is detrimental for your health, and it can lead to physical problems. If you have constant stress, then you can develop high blood pressure or digestive issues. Reduce stress by using coloring for stress relief. Rather than using food or alcohol to relieve your stress after a difficult workday, keep an assortment of coloring pages and beautiful crayons ready at home.

SELF LOVE is your SUPER power

DECODED MESSAGE
GOLDEN THOUGHTS

" |_|_|_|_|_| |_|_|_|_|_|_|_|_|_|
|_|_|_|_|_|_|_| |_|_|_|_| |_|_|
|_|_|_|_|_|_| |_|_|_|_|_| |_|_|_|
|_|_|_|_|_| |_|_|_|_|_|_|_|_|_|_|_|_|,
_	_	_	_	_	_	_		_	_	_
_	_	_	_	_	_	_	,	_	_	_		_	_	_	'_	_
_	_	_	_	_	_		_	_	_	_	_
_	_	_	_	_	_		_	_	_	_	_		_	_	_
_	_	_		_	_	_		_	_	_	_	_	_	!

here enter the deciphered message for you ↱

Golden thoughts.

SOLVE THE MAZE AND YOU WILL DECODE THE MESSAGE

FINISH

START

n	!	e	h	W	!	W	h		s	n	o	n	e		s	t	a	b	s		y
i	e	h	W	!	n	!	e	n		s	e	o	n	e		s	t	a	b	y	o	u
a	g	W	!	n	i	W	h	e	n		m	e	o	n	e		s	t	a	b	u
g	a	g	W	!	a	h	e	n		s	o	m	e	o	n	e		a	o	y	o	u
a		t		a	g	a	n		s	o	m	e	o	n	e		a	b	s		y	o
t	i		t		a	g	a	i	n	!	e	o	n	e	t		s	t	a	b	y	o	u
t		i		t	g	a	i	n	i	n	o	n	e		s		d	a	b	s	o	u
	t	o		a	g	a	g	a	i	n	e		t	o		d	o		i	t
	o	d	o		i	t		a	g	a	a		k		t	o		d	o		i	t
t	o		d	o		i	a	a	c	k	b	k	c	k		t	o		d	o		i
	t	d	o		t		b		e		c	a	c	k		t	o		d	o
k		o		i	e	f	a	f	i	f	e		b	a	c	k		t	d		i
c	k		i	b	f	i	n	k	n	i	f	e		c	k		d	i	t		e
a	b	a	e		i	n	k		k	n	i	f	e	k		t	o		i	t		f
b		e	f	i	n	k		e		k	n	i		c	k		d	o		i	i
o	m	e	o	n	e		t	h	e		i	f	b	a	c	t	o		d	o	i	n
s	e	o	n	e	t	s		t	h	k	n	i	a	c	k		t	o	e		k
	s	n	e		a	t	m	e		k	f	e		h	i	m		t	h	e
n		s	t	s	t	a	i	m		k	n	i	v	e		h	i	t		t	h	e
e		n		a	s	b	h		h	v	i	g	i	v	e		h	p	t		t	h	t
h	e	s	o	y		s		e	v	i	g		g	i	v	c	c	e	p	t		t
W	h	e	n	o	y		y	o	o	v	i	t		a	c	a	c	c	e	p	t		t
h	e	n	n	i	o	y	d		d	o	n	'	t			,		a	c	c	e	p	t
e	n		i		u	o	u	t	e	c	c	a		,	s	,		a	c	c	e	p
h	t		n	i		u	b	u	p	t	h	c	a	c	e	s	,		a	c	c	e
e	h	t		n	i			t	t		t		t	h	z	e	s	,		a	c	c
	e	h	e	h	t	i		,	o	p	t	h	d	h	e		i	z	e	s	,		a	c
b		e	h	t		n	y	,	a		e	n	d	n		g	i	z	e	s	,		a
a	b		e	h	t		g	o	p	a		a	n		o	g	i	z	e	s	,
c	a	b		e	h	t	o	l	o	p	k		a	a	l	o	g	i	z	,		a
k	c	a	b		e	h	e		b	a	c	a	n	p	o	l	o	g	e		c	c

TAKE CARE OF YOUR RESOURCES TO BECOME STRONGER

There's a huge difference between spending time and investing it. The word "spending" means that you're using something up or exhausting it. When you spend time, you're not really looking to get anything back. When you invest in something you expend resources, but you do so with an expectation of getting a good return on your investment (ROI). Investing your time means that you engage in activities which are calculated to bring you meaningful rewards.

"Investing" and "ROI" are terms which, up until now, you've probably heard only when it comes to money. However, you should start thinking of these terms when it comes to your time & energy, as well.

You can invest your valuable time and energy in mental and personal development, health, creating a future, building a business, developing passions.

The best investment is an investment in yourself.

It's time to invest your time, money and energy in what matters most – yourself.

It's all up to you, take your time to create an investment plan and put it into action as soon as possible, determine the benefits you will achieve after 90 days.

EXAMPLES

TIME & ENERGY INVESTMENT PLAN

PURPOSE	DESCRIPTION	HOW OFTEN	HOW MUCH TIME I WILL INVEST IN 90 DAYS
extra income	I will devote time each day to building an additional source of income	2 hours a day	(2 hours x 90 days) 180 hours
health	Every day I will invest my time in practicing yoga	30 minutes a day	45 hours
personal development	I will invest time in reading books on personal development	4 times a week for an hour each	52 hours

SUMMARY: IN 90 DAYS, I INVESTED 277 HOURS IN MYSELF

TIME & ENERGY
INVESTMENT PLAN
FOR 90 DAYS

PURPOSE	DESCRIPTION	HOW OFTEN	HOW MUCH TIME I WILL INVEST IN 90 DAYS

TIME & ENERGY
INVESTMENT PLAN
FOR 90 DAYS

PURPOSE	DESCRIPTION	HOW OFTEN	HOW MUCH TIME I WILL INVEST IN 90 DAYS

COLORING THERAPY

3 / 15

Mental stress is detrimental for your health, and it can lead to physical problems. If you have constant stress, then you can develop high blood pressure or digestive issues. Reduce stress by using coloring for stress relief. Rather than using food or alcohol to relieve your stress after a difficult workday, keep an assortment of coloring pages and beautiful crayons ready at home.

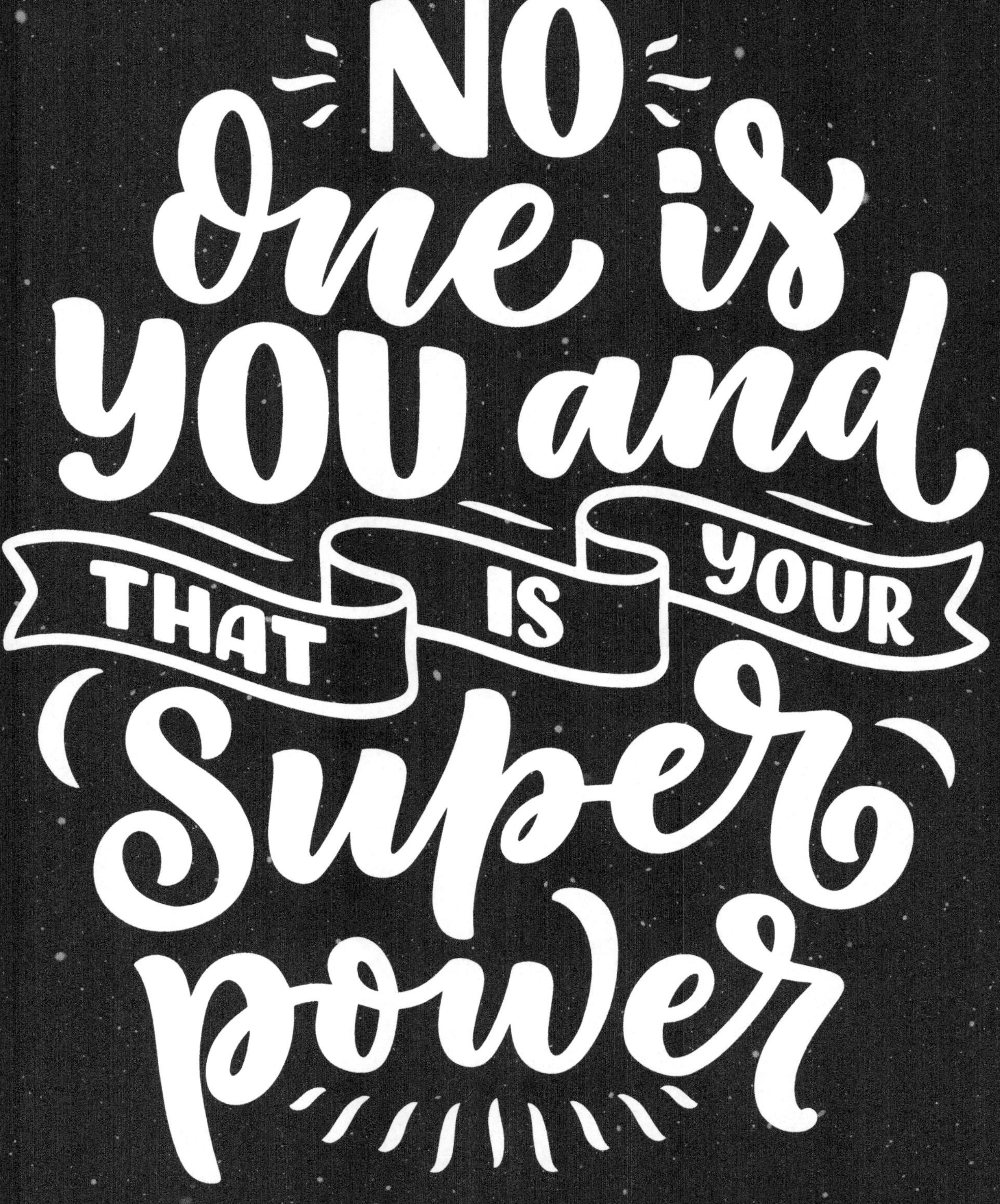

NO
one is
YOU and
THAT   IS   YOUR
super
power

WORDS OF LOVE

GOODWILL
CELEBRATION
LOVERS
INDULGENCE
PARTNERSHIP
FRIENDSHIP
FAVOR
UNDERSTANDING
LONGING
HAPPINESS
HARMONY
AFFECTION
ROMANTICISM
CHOICE
INFATUATION
KINDNESS
FAITHFULNESS
RESPECT
SACRIFICE
COOPERATION
DESIRE
LOYALTY
BALANCE
SUPPORT
FAMILY
PASSION
TRUST
SATISFACTION
CRAVING
COMPATIBILITY
FEELING
LOVING
TENDERNESS
DEVOTION

Words of Love.

You are in for a tough job - you can handle it if you are persistent. Find the words associated with true love in all the clutter. Focus all your attention on these wonderful words and find them. If you can handle it - you can handle anything. When you're done, take a moment to think about how many of these words are familiar to you - how many you've experienced, how many you haven't, and how many you want to experience in the future.

```
S Y R G T I M O H C T E S A H Q M R I P G N I J C M B R O Z
O S L Q N D F C O C E U T Z S G R V O L C N O U H F O K O L
H A E I L A Q O N Y M Y F G E V V W J M F E W P O A K U Y P
R K C N M X Y M R J Y S Y J D G U J Z A A C O I I Q K R U B
O A Z H L A Y M A F E X V A Q K B Z T H N N K S C V T K U U
E U C V S U F O A F F E C T I O N U M Q S E T A E M U R L X
I X V Q K W F N E L W C I H J R A P Q J C G D I T V E D A V
T F P J Q D V H W O F Z H S C T I H G Q I L T W C I C I C A
S S E N D N I K T P H T M U I H N X D E T U Q F X I Y I W Z
T J H H K X I A V I S S B O S H G Y V B C D H H A O S T C B
Q L T P E Y K P L U A N R P P S C P V C N S P R V H M A W
Y T R O P P U S R D Z F E X Z M O L E E J I S Q S I O L K I
J X M A C O W T L S Y N A F V P A Q N B B A E N F A A R K U
Z R X P O L K P Y O T Q B I I N M J A R J B N P V N O X L Z
D L Y U U G B X C R V B G T S S O I X Y Q B I R C V J L N W
V E L L K K N W A K G Y O U B O X O R X T G P E L Q D X P D
S X S J K V Z P K E Z Q B Y C O Y O Y M F B P I Y A B V K F
I R G I M W L H C O O K V H B Q N N O M Z L A C J V E N T O
L Z E J R U J I E L B H V T S G O X Y J M S H M G Y X W C O
L P F V R E F H N C D N N M J M W G V J F C E G O Y W S E I
O B L I O I L G O X Z H F O R W E C Q N T D P I N D G S P X
Y J Y A R L O J I Q C L Y A C O O P E R A T I O N I D S S J
A V Q C G O V Z S F X Q H K M F I F J D Q O I E C F G G E B
L T A B D K N P S Y L P A F Q E N X X B W Q G J N O X N R T
T S Q W F X N W A S H V E G V U S E F R I E N D S H I P O D
Y Q I Q G Y N X P W L X J S N D P C J O A J X T P K N O A L
N L B B A R F J R C W C R J B Z N A P Z X S Q U N V Q U U L
L C H R E E N Y Q J Z E Q U T S I S F O E V F U Z B O B H G
N O I T A R B E L E C G N I D N A T S R E D N U G R H A H E
W N C L L W D X Y D W V Y U G J E I H N X H E J V H O R L C
```

YOUR

POEM

DECODED MESSAGE
GOLDEN THOUGHTS

here enter the deciphered message for you

Solve the rebus and decipher the hidden message

DOG G=N+' TV -V

CD D=R+Y

BELL -LL + CAR R=U+ ROSE -RO

I+ TV -V='+S

LOVE -L+ RAT -AT+.

SKI K=M+ LEFT -FT

BEAR -AR+ CAR B=U+ ROSE -RO

I+ TV -V

HAT T=P+ YEN y=P+ CD C=E

COLORING THERAPY

4 / 15

Mental stress is detrimental for your health, and it can lead to physical problems. If you have constant stress, then you can develop high blood pressure or digestive issues. Reduce stress by using coloring for stress relief. Rather than using food or alcohol to relieve your stress after a difficult workday, keep an assortment of coloring pages and beautiful crayons ready at home.

Selfcare IS NOT SELFISH

ART
THERAPY

Color the picture using as many colors as possible

Color the picture using as many colors as possible

SELF-CARE CHECKLIST

- ☐ Good sleep
- ☐ Meditate
- ☐ Exercise
- ☐ Read book
- ☐ Eat healthy
- ☐ Drink more water

There is no more important thing in life than taking care of yourself. It is a priority in life. The more you take care of yourself, the more you will love and respect yourself. Taking care of yourself and your body requires regularity. Create your daily plan to take care of yourself and do your best to follow it every day. No one and nothing is or will ever be more important than taking care of yourself. Only you can do it, only you are responsible for it. Keep yourself in good shape. This is your most important task.

If you start taking care of yourself and respecting your body others will too.

Daily Self-Care Checklist

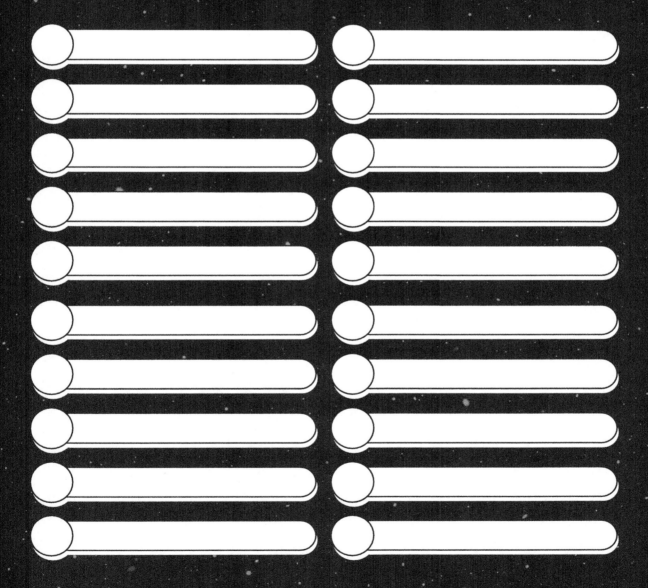

COLORING THERAPY

5 / 15

Mental stress is detrimental for your health, and it can lead to physical problems. If you have constant stress, then you can develop high blood pressure or digestive issues. Reduce stress by using coloring for stress relief. Rather than using food or alcohol to relieve your stress after a difficult workday, keep an assortment of coloring pages and beautiful crayons ready at home.

SELF-
AWARENESS

Self-awareness activities and exercises are tools that can help you to not only reach your goals but also to discover who you are at core level and what you want out of life.

The more you 'peel the onion' per se, the more you will discover what lies underneath. Self-awareness and self-improvement go hand in hand.

Becoming more self-aware can help you understand your wants, needs, and desires as well as your strengths and weaknesses.

Self-awareness is also an important tool for success. Those internal mental processes guide how you behave and how you act. When you become more self-aware, you begin uncovering those destructive thought patterns and unhealthy habits.

These questions are designed to make you think. Answering these questions is a powerful method of self-discovery.

72

Self-awareness
Questions on personality:

1. Describe yourself in three words.

2. Is your personality like either of your parents?

YES ○
○ NO

3. Ask yourself if your personality has changed since childhood?

YES ○
○ NO

4. What things scare you?

5. What qualities do you most admire in yourself?

6. How would you complete the question: "What if?".

7. Do you make decisions logically or intuitively?

logical ☐
intuitive ☐

Self-awareness Questions on relationships:

1. Describe your ideal intimate relationship.

2. Who would you call if you only had a few minutes to live? What would you say?

3. Describe a devastating moment in terms of relationships.

4. Ask yourself if you treat yourself better than others?

5. Of all the relationships you have had, describe the best moment.

Self-awareness Qquestions on values and life goals:

1. What does your ideal "you" look like?

2. What kinds of dreams and goals do you have?

3. Rank 5-10 of the most important things in your life in your career, family, relationships and love, money, etc.

4. Of all the relationships you have had, describe the best moment.

COLORING THERAPY

6 / 15

Mental stress is detrimental for your health, and it can lead to physical problems. If you have constant stress, then you can develop high blood pressure or digestive issues. Reduce stress by using coloring for stress relief. Rather than using food or alcohol to relieve your stress after a difficult workday, keep an assortment of coloring pages and beautiful crayons ready at home.

DECODED MESSAGE
GOLDEN THOUGHTS

"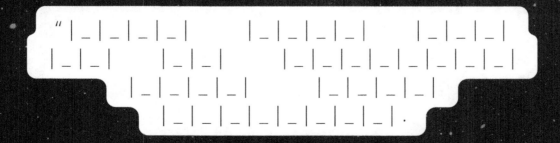

here enter the deciphered message for you

Solve the rebus and decipher the hidden message.

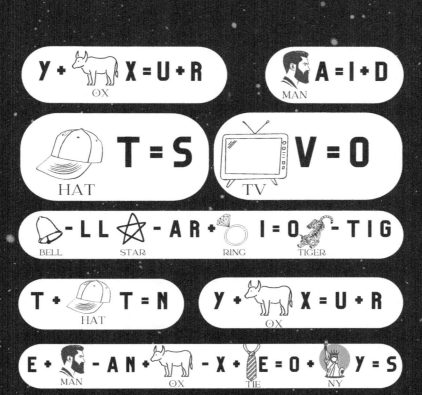

Y + OX X = U + R

MAN A = I + D

HAT T = S

TV V = O

BELL - LL STAR - AR + RING I = O TIGER - TIG

T + HAT T = N

Y + OX X = U + R

E + MAN - AN + OX - X + TIE E = O + NY Y = S

COLORING THERAPY

7 / 15

Mental stress is detrimental for your health, and it can lead to physical problems. If you have constant stress, then you can develop high blood pressure or digestive issues. Reduce stress by using coloring for stress relief. Rather than using food or alcohol to relieve your stress after a difficult workday, keep an assortment of coloring pages and beautiful crayons ready at home.

THE
POWER
OF
WORDS

by Habib Sadeghi, excerpted from
The Clarity Cleanse

...rds have tremendous power, and ...ether their effects are positive or ...ative depends on how we choose ...use them. I can't express how ...erful a tool free-form writing is ...expel negative energy from our ...ds and hearts. I used it daily ...ing my recovery from cancer. I ...return to it whenever I'm feeling ...tionally oversaturated. No matter ...t's happening in our lives or what ...dition we suffer from, I firmly ...eve in the transformative power ...riting to heal us from the inside

I'm not the only one who believes this. It's one of the reasons people have kept diaries and journals for generations. There's also ample scientific research to back up the idea. As psychologist Karen Baikie and psychiatrist Kay Wilhelm wrote in their article "Emotional and Physical Health Benefits of Expressive Writing" (Advances in Psychiatric Treatment, August 2005).

Over the past 20 years, a growing body of literature has demonstrated the beneficial effects that writing about traumatic or stressful events has on physical and emotional health...The immediate impact of expressive writing is usually a short-term increase in distress, negative mood and physical symptoms, and a decrease in positive mood compared with controls. Expressive writing participants also rate their writing as significantly more personal, meaningful and emotional. However, at longer-term follow-up, many studies have continued to find evidence of health benefits in terms of objectively assessed outcomes, self-reported physical health outcomes and self-reported emotional health outcomes.

Those kinds of benefits to our physical and emotional health are what we're aiming for with the PEW 12 exercise. Here's how it works. Every emotion has a charge, and the positive or negative energy an emotion generates has a real and measurable impact on our bodies. The act of writing allows us to physically release some of that charge much in the same way we release tension during sex. Burning the page, which happens at the end of the exercise, allows us to purge even more of that charge and serves as a symbol of letting go. If you can release negative energy on a regular basis, it doesn't accumulate. You could look at this exercise as an act of freedom. Whenever you release your emotions, you lighten your burden so you don't have to carry it with

This exercise works best if you just keep writing and don't stop to think about what you'll write next or self-edit. Forget about punctuation or making your handwriting pretty, even legible. In fact you may get to the point where your emotions are flowing so fast and furiously that you can't even write real words. That's great. Just keep the pen in contact with the paper and let the thoughts roll out of you. This isn't a time to be polite or fair. This is your side of the story. Also, at the end of the exercise you'll be destroying the pages you've written, so as you write there's no reason to worry about anyone else reading them.

AFFIRMATIONS FOR LOVE

Some people get disappointed in love when they've got their heart broken, or when they give love but they don't receive it back. Another reason is when they get betrayed or let down. Everyone deserves to have a happy, healthy, and loving relationship in order to experience the happiness, joy, and fulfillment of giving and receiving love.

If you've recently got through a breakup, or you just haven't met your soulmate yet, this set of loving affirmations can help to open your heart and put you in a state of attracting love energy, and attract the right person for you.

You may find yourself wondering what are affirmations, and whether or not they work, which is totally understandable.

Put simply, positive affirmations are statements that you make to yourself, which reinforce a positive aspect of your life. They are powerful tools that take positive statements to help overcome negative thoughts and allow you to focus on the good things in life.

Create your own love affirmation or use ready-made inspirations. Repeat it every day until it comes true.

Good affirmation has five basic ingredients:

- It's personal.
- It's positive.
- It's present tense.
- It's visual.
- It's emotional.

For example: "I (personal) love (emotional) the positive energy (positive) that love brings (present tense). And then you can visualize it.

Pick 3-8 loving affirmations that deeply resonate with you and repeat them daily. Spend a few minutes each day and totally relax your mind and body.

You can also practice these positive love affirmations with journaling, and/or meditating.
If you do this, day by day your behavior will change.
You'll start to get into the mindset of love, appreciating every small act of love, where before you wouldn't even notice.

Ready-made love affirmations

- The universe wants to bring me, my perfect partner.
- The right person is on their way, and they are worth waiting for.
- Someone out there is ready to love me just as I am, and appreciate me.
- I am attracting a relationship with trust and mutual respect.
- When I meet that special person, everything will just fall into place.
- I am attracting a lasting relationship.
- I am attracting my soulmate.
- Someone is looking for a special person just like me. It's just a matter of time.
- I believe in my ability to attract my soulmate.
- I am ready to share life with my soulmate.
- I naturally attract loving and healthy relationships into my life.
- I am unconditionally loving.
- My heart is open to finding love.
- All the love I need is already within me.
- Today, I am choosing to be loved.
- I attract and manifest love easily and effortlessly.
- I love life, and life loves me back.
- Now that I love myself, others love me too.
- I am loved fully and completely.
- I radiate love from within.
- I am worthy of deep, maningful love.
- I commit to letting love into my life now.
- I release any fears and resistances around being loved now.
- I am open to giving my pure love.
- There are countless opportunities to meet my love.
- I trust the universe to send me my ideal match.
- I am relaxed and ready to receive love.
- I deserve love and happiness. Finding love is easy.
- I attract naturally loving relationships in my life
- I am loved more than I ever

- I feel the love of others who are not around me.
- I am an amazing gift to myself, my friends, and the world. I am too much of an amazing gift to feel self-pity.
- I love and appreciate myself. I am who I am and I love myself.
- I do not need the company of others to feel complete. I am more than enough. I enjoy being in my own solitude.
- The past no longer matters. It has no control over me. What only matters is the present. What I do in the present will shape my future. The past has no say in this.
- Everything that I need will be provided to me at the right time and the right place. When something is meant to happen it will happen.
- It is too early to give up on my dreams. it is always too early to give up on my dreams.
- I will not give up until I have tried everything. And when I have tried everything I will look for other ways to try.
- I believe in myself and I believe in the path I have chosen. I cannot choose the obsticles in my way, but I can choose to continue on my path, because it leads to my goals.
- I am not only enough, I am more than enough. I also get better every day I live. Tomorrow I will be a better version of myself than I was today.
- I will not criticize myself. I will love myself for who I am and for what I have become.
- I will award and praise myself for my accomplishments. I will not dwell on the praise of others for my own praise is more than enough.
- I will not compare myself to anyone else because everyone is on their own personal journeys. My journey is unique and cannot be compared.
- I will only compare myself to myself. I know what greatness I can accomplish and I will only hold myself to that.

DECODED MESSAGE

GOLDEN THOUGHTS

★ ★ ★ ★ ★

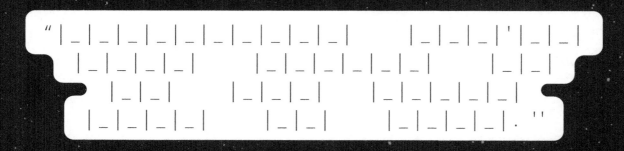

"|_|_|_|_|_|_|_|_|_|_|_| |_|_|_|_|'|_|_|
|_|_|_|_| |_|_|_|_|_|_|_| |_|_|
|_|_| |_|_| |_|_|_|_|_|
|_|_|_|_| |_|_| |_|_|_|_|_|."

here enter the deciphered message for you ↗

Solve the rebus and decipher the hidden message.

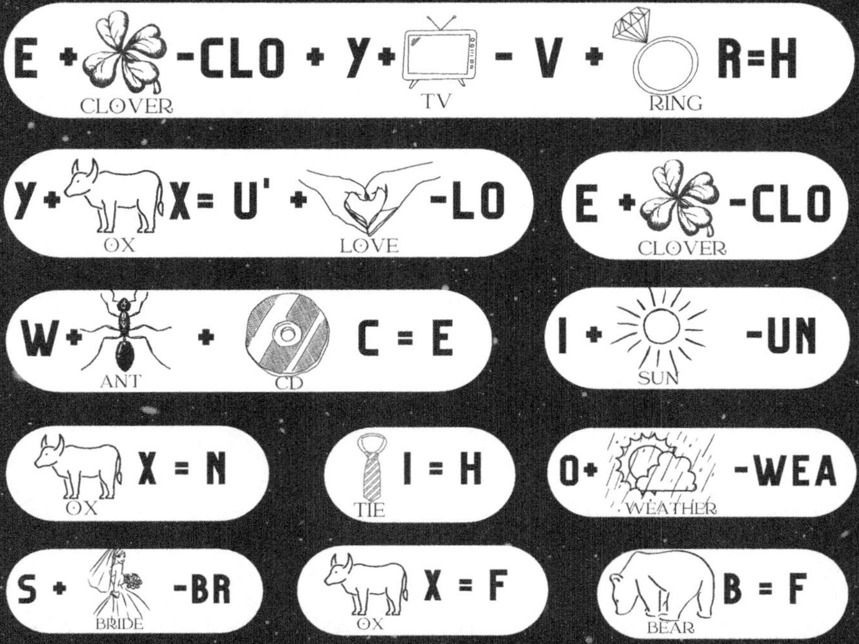

E + CLOVER -CLO + Y + TV - V + RING R=H

Y + OX X= U' + LOVE -LO

E + CLOVER -CLO

W + ANT + CD C = E

I + SUN -UN

OX X = N

TIE I = H

O + WEATHER -WEA

S + BRIDE -BR

OX X = F

BEAR B = F

COLORING THERAPY

8 / 15

Mental stress is detrimental for your health, and it can lead to physical problems. If you have constant stress, then you can develop high blood pressure or digestive issues. Reduce stress by using coloring for stress relief. Rather than using food or alcohol to relieve your stress after a difficult workday, keep an assortment of coloring pages and beautiful crayons ready at home.

SELF CARE

BIGGEST
DREAM

COLOR
THERAPY
SHADES OF GREEN

Color the picture using only
shades of green.

COLORING THERAPY

9 / 15

Mental stress is detrimental for your health, and it can lead to physical problems. If you have constant stress, then you can develop high blood pressure or digestive issues. Reduce stress by using coloring for stress relief. Rather than using food or alcohol to relieve your stress after a difficult workday, keep an assortment of coloring pages and beautiful crayons ready at home.

RESIST
RETALIATING

Resist retaliating.

With some betrayals, you may experience an overwhelming
urge to retaliate. **Don't!**

You may be feeling angry about what happened and you may
feel like they deserve punishment, but rarely is this ever a
productive endeavor. If there's one way to prolong the hurt
and delay the healing process, it's by plotting and planning
your revenge. Instead of taking revenge, vent your anger on
this piece of paper.

**You can tear this sheet of paper, perforate it, trample it, blur
or color the picture.**

COLORING THERAPY

10 / 15

Mental stress is detrimental for your health, and it can lead to physical problems. If you have constant stress, then you can develop high blood pressure or digestive issues. Reduce stress by using coloring for stress relief. Rather than using food or alcohol to relieve your stress after a difficult workday, keep an assortment of coloring pages and beautiful crayons ready at home.

Color the picture & Relax.

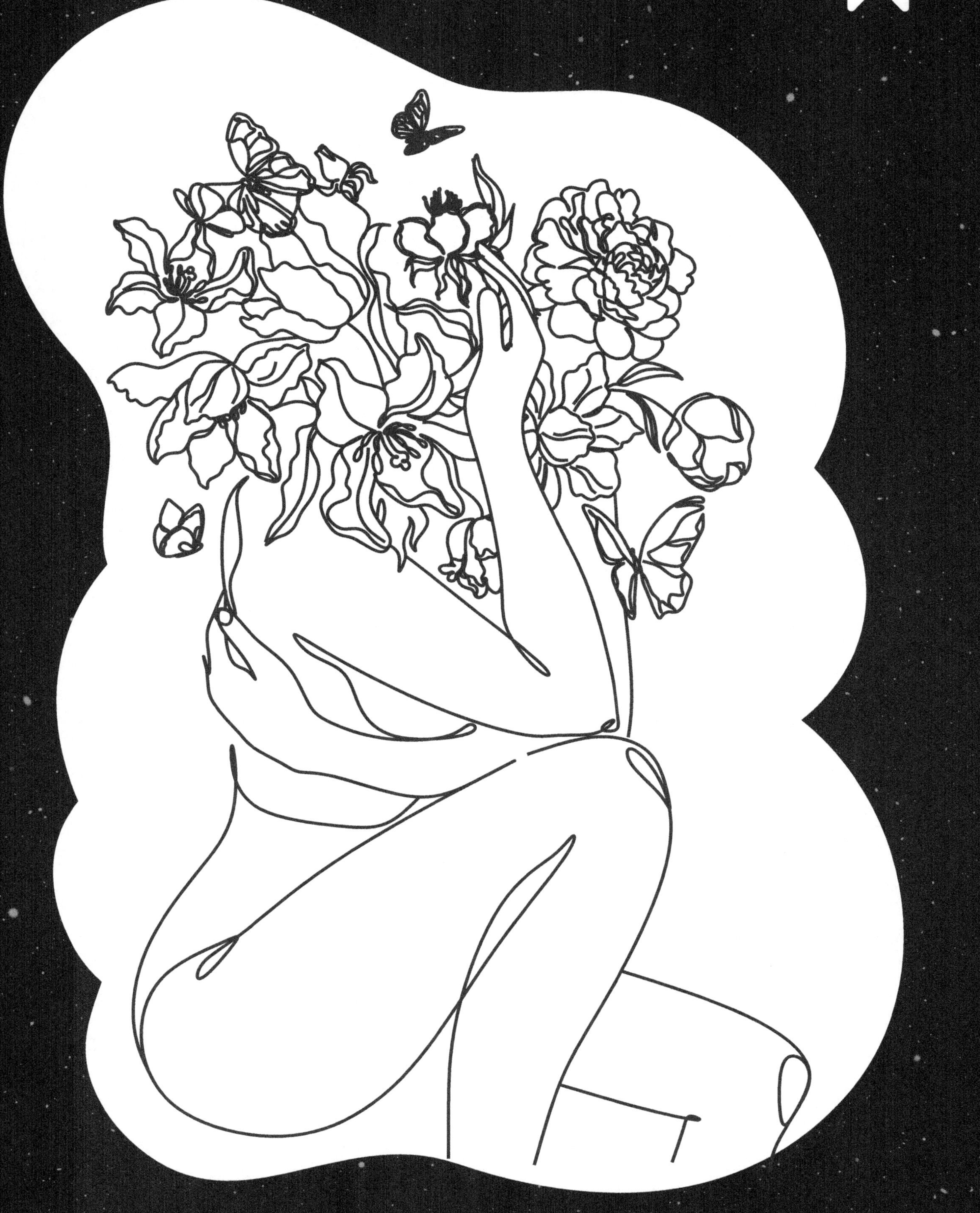

HIERARCHY OF VALUES

Life offers infinite variety, along with myriad challenges and opportunities. It's easy to get lost in indecision with so many choices. You'd like to have balance in your life, but there are so many conflicts that you often find yourself spending energy too much in one direction.

What's happening here is a lack of prioritization, of figuring out what in life is most important to you — and then acting upon it. While not life-threatening, a failure to identify what's most meaningful to you can erode your quality of living. To ensure that you have the most opportunities to live a full, happy and productive life, you must zero in on your key priorities. One way to determine one's pyrrhotites is to establish one's own hierarchy of values. Cut out and organize values and priorities placing the most important ones at the top.

Establish your own hierarchy of values.
Values and pririties to be cut out are at the back of the book, you can
also create your own.

Health

Trust   Love

Happiness   Creativity   Balance

Empathy   Compassion   Acceptance   Awareness

Knowledge   Calmness   Freedom   Innovation   Discipline

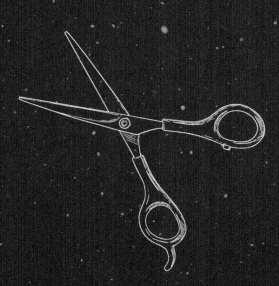

JOUR-
NAL-
ING

Keep your journal for a week. Write down your thoughts and reflections in it every day. After 7 days: analyze the written thoughts.

When you journal, the act of taking a thought and putting it onto paper gives you the ability to really see it and examine it. This process neutralizes the thought from any extra emotions, or judgment it might be carrying and gives you the power to decide what to do with the thought. You can choose to keep the thought, to re-write, or rewire the thought to be similar, but more positive, or to push the thought away and uninvite it into your brain.

The act of taking pen to paper is perhaps the most life-giving foundational strategy for anyone who wants to master their mindset.

DAY
1

DAILY JOURNAL

MON   TUE   WED   THU   FRI   SAT   SUN

○   ○   ○   ○   ○   ○   ○

DATE: _____

DAY 2

DAILY JOURNAL

MON   TUE   WED   THU   FRI   SAT   SUN
○   ○   ○   ○   ○   ○   ○

DATE: _____

DAY
3

DAILY JOURNAL

MON   TUE   WED   THU   FRI   SAT   SUN
○   ○   ○   ○   ○   ○   ○

DATE: _____

DAY
4

DAILY JOURNAL

MON TUE WED THU FRI SAT SUN
○   ○   ○   ○   ○   ○   ○

DATE: _____

DAY
5

DAILY JOURNAL

MON   TUE   WED   THU   FRI   SAT   SUN
○   ○   ○   ○   ○   ○   ○

DATE: _____

DAY
6

DAILY JOURNAL

MON   TUE   WED   THU   FRI   SAT   SUN

○   ○   ○   ○   ○   ○   ○

DATE: _____

DAY
7

DAILY JOURNAL

MON   TUE   WED   THU   FRI   SAT   SUN

○   ○   ○   ○   ○   ○   ○

DATE: _____

COLORING THERAPY

11 / 15

Mental stress is detrimental for your health, and it can lead to physical problems. If you have constant stress, then you can develop high blood pressure or digestive issues. Reduce stress by using coloring for stress relief. Rather than using food or alcohol to relieve your stress after a difficult workday, keep an assortment of coloring pages and beautiful crayons ready at home.

FIND YOUR WAY TO TRUE LOVE

Find your way to true love - it's not easy,
but you'll succeed because you deserve it.

IF YOU CAN GET THROUGH THIS MAZE,
YOU CAN DO ANYTHING

IT'S TIME
TO CLEAN UP

It's time to clean up. Get rid of things that remind you of the person who betrayed you. Have no mercy, throw away or give away all the things that you associate badly with you. Before you start color the picture and collect your thoughts

COLORING THERAPY

12 / 15

Mental stress is detrimental for your health, and it can lead to physical problems. If you have constant stress, then you can develop high blood pressure or digestive issues. Reduce stress by using coloring for stress relief. Rather than using food or alcohol to relieve your stress after a difficult workday, keep an assortment of coloring pages and beautiful crayons ready at home.

GET TO KNO

YOUR WEAKNESSES

YOURSELF

YOUR STRENGTHS

ADVANTAGES

PASSIONS

SKILLS

SUCCESSES

WHAT YOU ARE GOOD AT

COLORING THERAPY

13 / 15

Mental stress is detrimental for your health, and it can lead to physical problems. If you have constant stress, then you can develop high blood pressure or digestive issues. Reduce stress by using coloring for stress relief. Rather than using food or alcohol to relieve your stress after a difficult workday, keep an assortment of coloring pages and beautiful crayons ready at home.

EXPRESSING GRATITUDE

Create your own gratitude affirmations or use ready-made ones and repeat them daily, watch carefully how your life changes when you express gratitude.

Expressing gratitude is an important part of being happy. In fact, there are countless mental and physical benefits to being thankful on a daily basis. And one of the simplest ways to build this simple practice is use what are called "gratitude affirmations." An affirmation of gratitude is a way for you to start and end every day on a positive note. If you take a few minutes every day simply writing out what you are grateful for when you go to sleep at night, you will not only go to bed thinking grateful thoughts but also wake up starting them.

1.

2.

3.

4.

5.

- . I understand that today is a gift, and I will live it in this gratitude.
- I am thankful for the ability to grow in whatever way I choose today.
- I have food, water, and security as I wake up today. These are wonderful blessings to have.
- My family and friends support me, and I am grateful for their love.
- My coffee (or tea) reminds me that it can be the small things that create the most joy.
- I recognize the beauty of the outside sunrise, and nature as it wakes for the day.

COLORING THERAPY

14 / 15

Mental stress is detrimental for your health, and it can lead to physical problems. If you have constant stress, then you can develop high blood pressure or digestive issues. Reduce stress by using coloring for stress relief. Rather than using food or alcohol to relieve your stress after a difficult workday, keep an assortment of coloring pages and beautiful crayons ready at home.

GRIEVE

Allow yourself to mourn for 1 day. Dress in black and let the past die. When the mourning is over, allow yourself to start a new phase in life.

Part of the process of getting over what happened is to grieve. In some cases, that might mean grieving the relationship that has ended. In others, it might mean grieving the future you had imagined for yourself and this other person, regardless of whether you have managed to save the relationship.

This will involve anger and sadness certainly, but lots of other feelings too. You may even slip into a temporary depression. You need to feel these feelings rather than suppressing them.

You'll need to accept that what happened happened. This doesn't mean you have to be okay with it, but you do need to acknowledge that the act took place and that it led to a great deal of hurt.

COLORING THERAPY

15 / 15

Mental stress is detrimental for your health, and it can lead to physical problems. If you have constant stress, then you can develop high blood pressure or digestive issues. Reduce stress by using coloring for stress relief. Rather than using food or alcohol to relieve your stress after a difficult workday, keep an assortment of coloring pages and beautiful crayons ready at home.

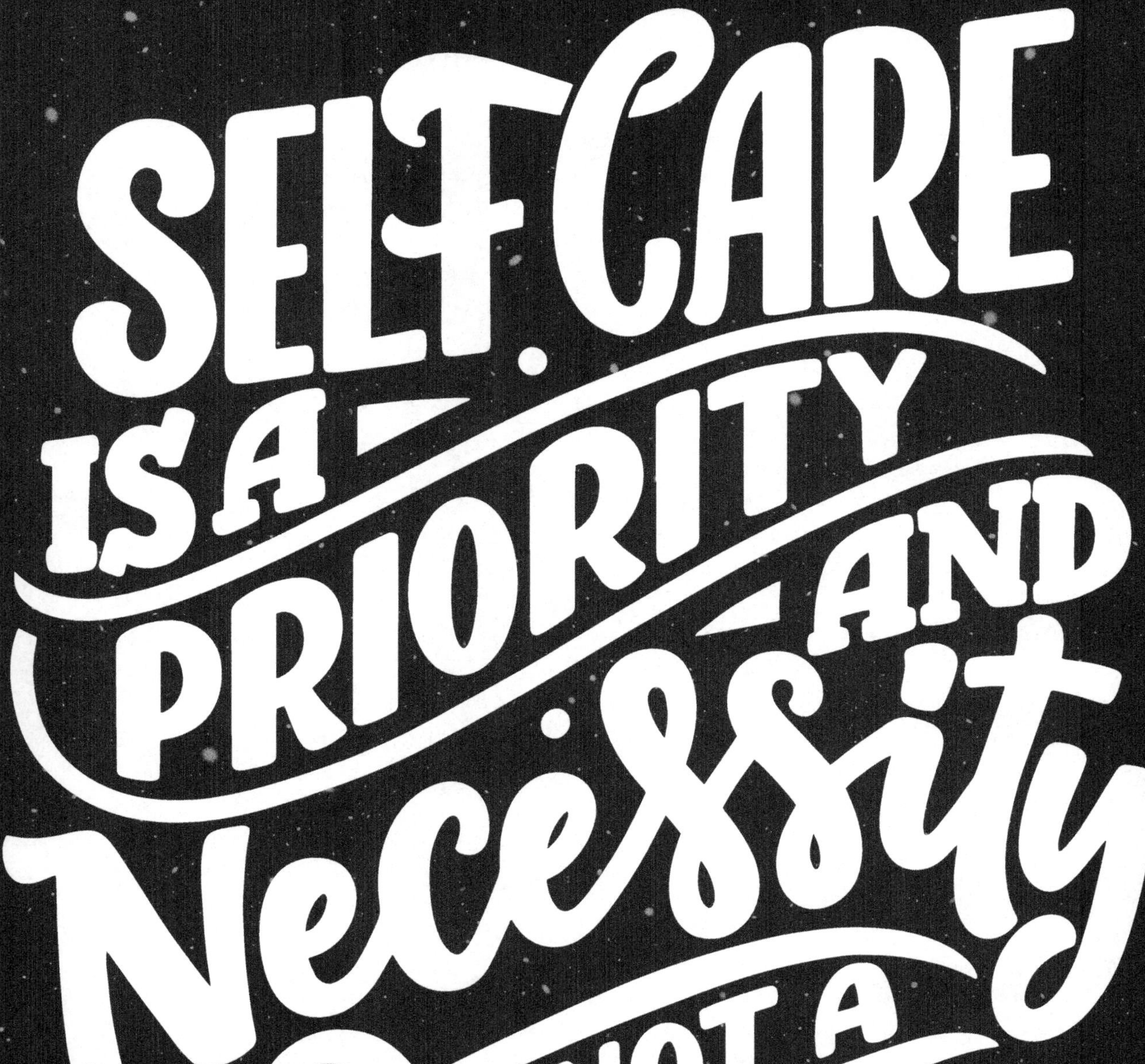
SELF CARE
IS A
PRIORITY
AND
Necessity
NOT A
LUXURY

Acceptance	Freedom
Adaptability	Gratitude
Awareness	Happiness
Balance	Health
Calmness	Humility
Community	Innovation
Creativity	Knowledge
Compassion	Leadership
Discipline	Love
Empathy	Trust

YOU made it!

If you have made it to the end of this book it is a sign that you are ready to start a new chapter in life. You have gotten to know yourself better, defined your boundaries and worked through the trauma of betrayal.

You have done the hard work on yourself, and you can be proud of it. Remember, however, that work on yourself lasts a lifetime. Never rest on your laurels. Love yourself and take care of yourself. This is your priority

You have undergone a transformation that you can share with others. I invite you to join a community of women who have experienced betrayal and have risen from the experience stronger, wiser and even more filled with love for themselves as well as others.

Share with us your experiences and feelings about processing this book. Perhaps your story will help other women who are currently in a situation like you were too.

Take a look at us on instagram and be sure to get back to us.

Charlotte Mia Legnano

And remember... true love always wins!
If it doesn't, know that it wasn't real.

@altered_by_betrayal

Printed in Great Britain
by Amazon

16078927R00086